Discovering Numbers

DISCOVERING NUMBERS

NEEPIN AUGER

RMB

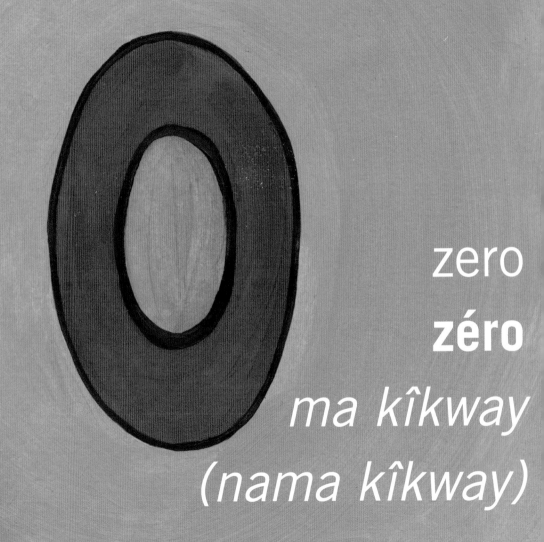

zero

zéro

ma kîkway

(nama kîkway)

one **un** *pêyak*

1

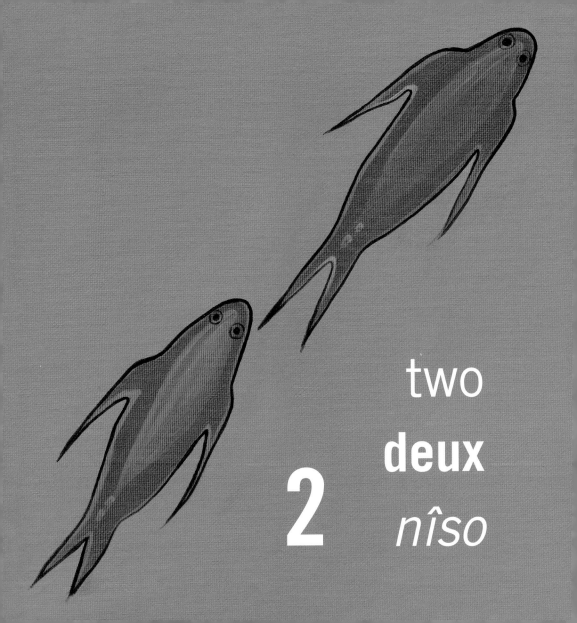

two

deux

2 *nîso*

3

three **trois** *nisto*

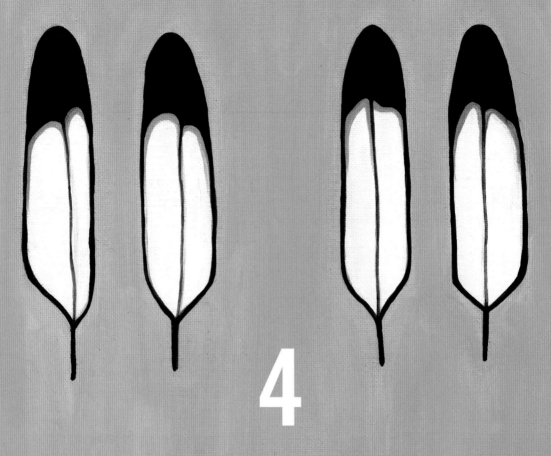

4

four **quatre** *nêwo*

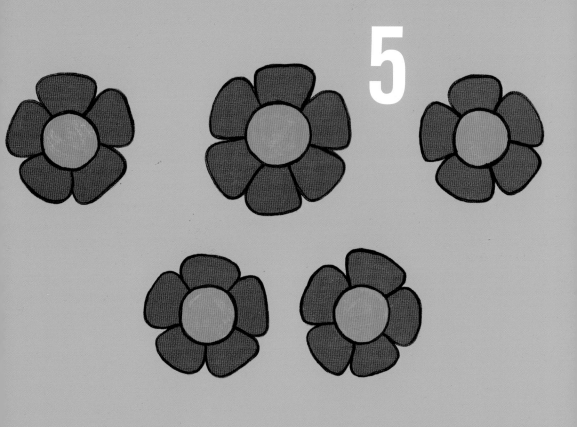

5

five **cinq** *niyânan*

6

six

six

nikotwâsik

7 seven **sept** *têpakohp*

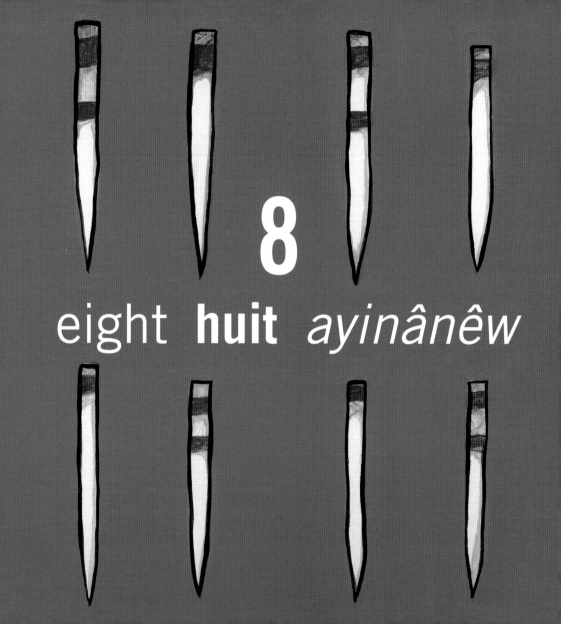

8

eight **huit** *ayinânêw*

9

nine **neuf** *kêkâ-mitâtâht*

10 ten **dix** *mitâtâht*

twenty **vingt** *nîsitanaw*

thirty **trente**

nistomitanaw

forty **quarante**

nêwomitanaw

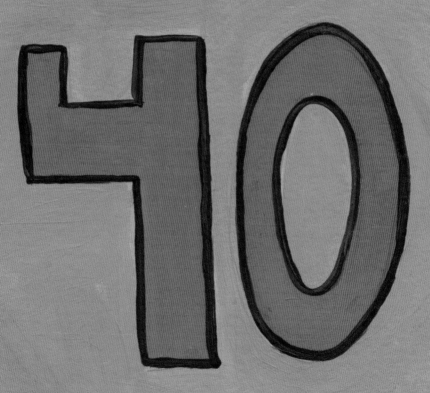

fifty **cinquante**

niyânanomitanaw

sixty **soixante**

nikotwâsomitanaw

seventy **soixante-dix**

têpakohpomitanaw

eighty **quatre-vingts**

ayênânêwomitanaw

ninety **quatre-vingt-dix**

kêkâ-mitâtahtomitanaw

one hundred **cent**

mitâtahtomitanaw

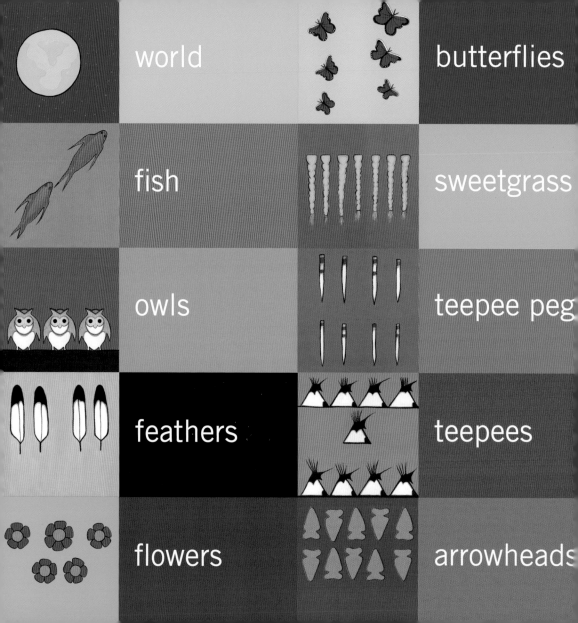

	world		butterflies
	fish		sweetgrass
	owls		teepee peg
	feathers		teepees
	flowers		arrowheads

20	30	40
50	60	70
80	90	100

Pronunciation Guide

0	zero (0)	zéro zeh-roh	ma kîkway (nama kîkway) mu keekway
1	one (world)	un ah	pêyak payuk
2	two (fish)	deux deuh	nîso neeso
3	three (owls)	trois twah	nisto nisto

4	four (feathers)	quatre	nêwo
		kat-reuh	naywo
5	five (flowers)	cinq	niyânan
		sank	neeyaanun
6	six (butterflies)	six	nikotwâsik
		see-s	nikotwaasik
7	seven (sweetgrass braids)	sept	têpakohp
		set	taypuhkohp
8	eight (teepee pegs)	huit	ayinânêw
		weet	uyinaanayoo
9	nine (teepees)	neuf	kêkâ-mitâtâht
		neuhf	kaykaa-mitaatuht

10	ten (arrowheads)	dix dee-s	mitâtâht mitaatuht
20	twenty (20)	vingt vahn	nîsitanaw neesitunaw
30	thirty (30)	trente tront	nistomitanaw nistomitunaw
40	forty (40)	quarante ka-ront	nêwomitanaw naywomitunaw
50	fifty (50)	cinquante sank-ont	niyânanomitanaw neeyaanunomitunaw

60	sixty (60)	soixante swa-sont	nikotwâsomitanaw nikotwaasomitunaw
70	seventy (70)	soixante-dix swa-sont-dee-s	têpakohpomitanaw taypuhkohpomitunaw
80	eighty (80)	quatre-vingts kat-reuh-vahn	ayênânêwomitanaw uyaynaanaywomitûnaw
90	ninety (90)	quatre-vingt-dix kat-reuh-vahn-dee-s	kêkâ-mitâtahtomitanaw kaykaa-mitaatuhtomitunaw
100	one hundred (100)	cent s-on	mitâtahtomitanaw mitaatuhtomitunaw

We would like to also take this opportunity to acknowledge the traditional territories upon which we live and work. In Calgary, Alberta, we acknowledge the Niitsitapi (Blackfoot) and the people of the Treaty 7 region in Southern Alberta, which includes the Siksika, the Piikuni, the Kainai, the Tsuut'ina and the Stoney Nakoda First Nations, including Chiniki, Bearpaw, and Wesley First Nations. The City of Calgary is also home to Métis Nation of Alberta, Region III. In Victoria, British Columbia, we acknowledge the traditional territories of the Lkwungen (Esquimalt, and Songhees), Malahat, Pacheedaht, Scia'new, T'Sou-ke and WSÁNEĆ (Pauquachin, Tsartlip, Tsawout, Tseycum) peoples.

For my daughter Gracie

Copyright © 2020 by Neepin Auger
First Paperback Edition, reprinted 2023

For information on purchasing bulk quantities of this book, or to obtain media excerpts or invite the author to speak at an event, please visit rmbooks.com and select the "Contact" tab.

RMB | Rocky Mountain Books Ltd.
rmbooks.com
@rmbooks
facebook.com/rmbooks

Cataloguing data available from Library and Archives Canada
ISBN 9781771604741 (paperback)
ISBN 9781771603317 (board book)
ISBN 9781771603324 (electronic)

Cree translations and pronunciations by Naomi McIlwraith and Cree Elder Elizabeth Letendre
French translations and pronunciations by David Warriner
Book design by Chyla Cardinal

Printed and bound in China

We acknowledge the financial support of the Government of Canada through the Canada Book Fund and the Canada Council for the Arts, and of the province of British Columbia through the British Columbia Arts Council and the Book Publishing Tax Credit.

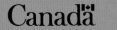

Canada Council
for the Arts

Conseil des Arts
du Canada

BRITISH
COLUMBIA

BRITISH COLUMBIA
ARTS COUNCIL
An agency of the Province of British Columbia